THE VIETNAM WAR
World Conflict Series

Written by Andrew Davis BA, B.ED

GRADES 5 - 8
Reading Levels 3 - 4

Classroom Complete Press
P.O. Box 19729
San Diego, CA 92159
Tel: 1-800-663-3609 | Fax: 1-800-663-3608
Email: service@classroomcompletepress.com

www.classroomcompletepress.com

ISBN-13: 978-1-55319-361-6
ISBN-10: 1-55319-361-x

© 2008

Critical Thinking Skills

The Vietnam War

Skills For Critical Thinking	Location and Geography?	Background and Causes	Major Figures	Major Battles	Weapons of War	The Role of the Navy	The War at Home	Remembering the War
LEVEL 1 Remembering								
• List Details/Facts			✓		✓		✓	✓
• Recall Information	✓	✓	✓	✓		✓	✓	
• Match Vocabulary to Definitions	✓	✓		✓	✓	✓		
• Recognize Validity(T/F)	✓	✓		✓	✓	✓		✓
LEVEL 2 Understanding								
• Summarize						✓		
• Describe					✓			
• Interpret	✓							
• Compare/Contrast		✓		✓	✓			✓
LEVEL 3 Applying								
• Use Outside Research Tools			✓	✓	✓		✓	✓
• Application to Own Life								✓
• Organize Facts			✓	✓		✓	✓	
• Apply Vocabulary Words in Sentences		✓			✓		✓	
LEVEL 4 Analysing								
• Draw Conclusions					✓	✓	✓	✓
• Make Inferences				✓		✓	✓	✓
LEVEL 5 Evaluating								
• State and Defend an Opinion	✓	✓		✓	✓		✓	✓
• Evaluate						✓		
• Explain		✓		✓	✓	✓	✓	✓
LEVEL 6 Creating								
• Imagine Self Interacting with Subject				✓				
• Create a Plan							✓	
• Imagine Alternatives							✓	

Based on Bloom's Taxonomy

Contents

🍎 **TEACHER GUIDE**

- Assessment Rubric 4
- How Is Our Resource Organized? 5
- Bloom's Taxonomy for Reading Comprehension 6
- Vocabulary 6

✏️ **STUDENT HANDOUTS**

- Reading Comprehension
  1. Location and Geography 7
  2. Background and Causes 10
  3. Major Figures 15
  4. Major Battles 20
  5. Weapons of the War 24
  6. The Role of the Navy 29
  7. The War at Home 33
  8. Remembering the War 37

- Hands-on Activities 42
- Crossword 46
- Word Search 47
- Comprehension Quiz 48

EZ✔ **EASY MARKING™ ANSWER KEY** 50
MINI POSTERS 55

✔ **6 BONUS Activity Pages!** Additional worksheets for your students

FREE!

- Go to our website: **www.classroomcompletepress.com/bonus**
- Enter item CC5506
- Enter pass code CC5506D

Assessment Rubric

The Vietnam War

Student's Name: _____ Assignment: _____ Level: _____

	Level 1	Level 2	Level 3	Level 4
Knowledge and Understanding	Demonstrates a limited understanding of content. Needs teacher assistance	Demonstrates a basic understanding of some of the content. Needs some teacher assistance	Demonstrates a good understanding of the content. Needs little teacher assistance	Demonstrates an excellent understanding of the content. No Teacher assistance needed
Inquiry and Research Skills	Able to answer questions about the text with limited effectiveness, not supported with proof from the text	Able to answer questions about the text with some effectiveness, supported with some proof from the text	Able to answer questions about the text with considerable effectiveness, supported with proof from the text	Able to answer questions about the text with a high degree of effectiveness, with excellent supporting proof from the text
Application and Making Connections	Limited application and interpretation in activities and responses, with few details	Basic application and interpretation in activities and responses, with some detail	Good application and interpretation in activities and responses, with a variety of details	Excellent application and interpretation in activities and responses, with a variety of concise details

STRENGTHS:

WEAKNESSES:

NEXT STEPS:

Teacher Guide

Our resource has been created for ease of use by both TEACHERS and STUDENTS alike.

Introduction

The Vietnam War was the longest military conflict in U.S. history. American involvement in Vietnam began in 1954 and ended in 1973 when the last troops were withdrawn. During the conflict more than 58,000 Americans lost their lives and more than 304,000 were wounded. The Vietnam War was also one of the most unpopular wars ever fought. Not since the Civil War had Americans been so divided.

Students will learn about the background and causes of the Vietnam War, major battles like Khe Sanh and Ia Drang, how major figures like Kennedy and Johnson shaped American policies in Vietnam, and how the War affected veterans and civilians at home. Our resource provides ready-to-use information and activities for remedial students in grades five to eight. Packed with reading passages, student activities, mini posters and fun exercises, this resource can be used effectively for whole-class, small group and independent work.

How Is Our Resource Organized?

STUDENT HANDOUTS

Reading passages and **activities** (*in the form of reproducible worksheets*) make up the majority of our resource. The reading passages present important grade-appropriate information and concepts related to the topic. Embedded in each passage are one or more questions that ensure students understand what they have read.

For each reading passage there are BEFORE YOU READ activities and AFTER YOU READ activities.

- The BEFORE YOU READ activities prepare students for reading by setting a purpose for reading. They stimulate background knowledge and experience, and guide students to make connections between what they know and what they will learn. Important concepts and vocabulary are also presented.

- The AFTER YOU READ activities check students' comprehension of the concepts presented in the reading passage and extend their learning. Students are asked to give thoughtful consideration of the reading passage through creative and evaluative short-answer questions, research, and extension activities.

The **Assessment Rubric** (*page 4*) is a useful tool for evaluating students' responses to many of the activities in our resource. The **Comprehension Quiz** (*page 48*) can be used for either a follow-up review or assessment at the completion of the unit.

PICTURE CUES

Our resource contains three main types of pages, each with a different purpose and use. A Picture Cue at the top of each page shows, at a glance, what the page is for.

 Teacher Guide
- Information and tools for the teacher

 Student Handouts
- Reproducible worksheets and activities

 Easy Marking™ Answer Key
- Answers for student activities

EASY MARKING™ ANSWER KEY
Marking students' worksheets is fast and easy with this **Answer Key**. Answers are listed in columns – just line up the column with its corresponding worksheet, as shown, and see how every question matches up with its answer!

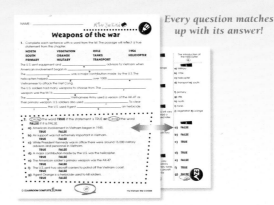

Every question matches up with its answer!

Bloom's Taxonomy

Our resource is an effective tool for any SOCIAL STUDIES PROGRAM.

Bloom's Taxonomy* for Reading Comprehension

The activities in our resource engage and build the full range of thinking skills that are essential for students' reading comprehension and understanding of important social studies concepts. Based on the six levels of thinking in Bloom's Taxonomy, and using language at a remedial level, information and questions are given that challenge students to not only recall what they have read, but move beyond this to understand the text and concepts through higher-order thinking. By using higher-order skills of applying, analysing, evaluating and creating, students become active readers, drawing more meaning from the text, and applying and extending their learning in more sophisticated ways.

Our resource, therefore, is an effective tool for any Social Studies program. Whether it is used in whole or in part, or adapted to meet individual student needs, our resource provides teachers with essential information and questions to ask, inspiring students' interest, creativity, and promoting meaningful learning.

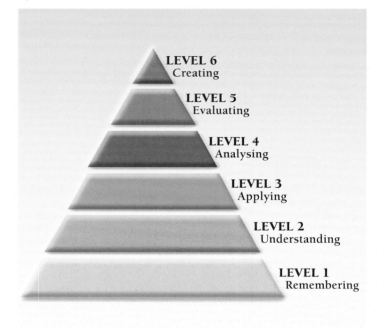

BLOOM'S TAXONOMY: 6 LEVELS OF THINKING

Bloom's Taxonomy is a widely used tool by educators for classifying learning objectives, and is based on the work of Benjamin Bloom.

Vocabulary

academy	combat	helicopter	occupied	support
advisors	communist	herbicide	operations	sweep
agricultural	congress	highlands	overthrown	sworn
aircraft	containment	independence	personnel	tanks
allies	continuous	information	political	terrain
ambushed	controlling	involvement	presidency	train
artillery	defeated	jungle	rainfall	troops
assassinated	deltas	lowlands	regiment	tropical
attacked	democracy	major	relieve	units
attrition	destroy	massive	reputation	warships
automatic	enemy	missions	resign	weapon
battle	equipment	mobility	resolution	withdrawal
climate	escalated	monsoon	senator	
coast	firepower	mortars	strategically	
colonial	government	murky	strikes	

Location and Geography

1. A. Mark the area on the map of the world where you think Vietnam is located.

B. Explain the reasons why you chose that spot.

_____

_____

C. Based on the area you chose on the map, what would be the temperature of a Vietnam winter?

_____

2. Can you name two common household items that are made in Vietnam today?

_____

3. A. Using the computer in your classroom pull up a map of the world and see how close you were to marking the correct spot of Vietnam.

B. Does this change your guess of what the temperature would be in the winter?

_____

Location and Geography

The country of Vietnam is located in Southeast Asia. It is a very long and narrow country shaped much like an "S". Vietnam is bordered on the east by the China Sea, on the north by China, and on the west by Cambodia and Laos. The whole country is around 1200 miles (1931.213 kilometers) from its' northern tip to the southern tip, and has an area of around 128,000 square miles (331518.478 square kilometers).

There are two major river deltas in Vietnam. One is in North Vietnam formed from the Red River, and the second is the Mekong delta in the south formed from the Mekong River. These two delta areas are the main agricultural growing areas in Vietnam. The main staple crop is rice, grown in vast rice paddies. Other agricultural products include coffee, tea, cashews, and rubber.

Vietnam is a country of great contrasts. The north consists mainly of highlands and the Red River Delta. The south consists of coastal lowlands, vast forests and dense jungle. A chain of mountains, called the Annamite Mountains, runs along almost the whole western border of the country.

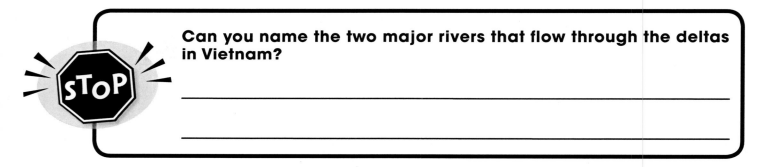

Can you name the two major rivers that flow through the deltas in Vietnam?

_____

_____

Vietnam has what is called a tropical monsoon climate. In the south the dry season runs from around November to April and has very hot temperatures. During the wet season there are large amounts of rainfall and it is not uncommon to have several days in a row of constant rain. In the north they also have a short winter season but the average temperature does not usually fall below 70 degrees fahrenheit (21 degrees celsius) in the daytime.

It was in this country of great contrasts that U.S. troops found themselves fighting. The terrain, along with the tropical climate, proved to be a real hurdle for the soldiers, vehicles, and equipment.

Location and Geography

1. (Circle) the word **TRUE** if the statement is TRUE **or** (Circle) the word **FALSE** if it is FALSE.

a) A typical Vietnam winter would be 32 degrees fahrenheit (0 degrees celcius).

   TRUE   FALSE

b) One of the main crops grown in Vietnam is rice.

   TRUE   FALSE

c) Vietnam consists of both highlands and lowlands.

   TRUE   FALSE

d) Rice crops are mainly grown in the deltas.

   TRUE   FALSE

e) The U.S. troops had no problems adapting to the climate.

   TRUE   FALSE

2. Match the Words below with the correct statement.

| WESTERN | RED | CHINA | VIETNAM | DRY | MONSOON |

[_____] **a)** Vietnam borders on this sea.

[_____] **b)** One of the main Rivers in North Vietnam is known as this.

[_____] **c)** Southeast Asia is where the location of this country is.

[_____] **d)** The Annamite Mountains run along this border.

[_____] **e)** The tropical climate in Vietnam is known as this.

[_____] **f)** November to April is very hot and is also known to be this.

3. (Circle) the word that does not belong in each line found below.

a) Lowlands, Mountains, Delta, Snow.

b) Sea, Hill, Ocean, River.

c) Rice, Cashews, Computer, Rubber.

NAME: _____

Background and Causes

1. Can you explain the difference between a Communist Government and a Democratic Government?

_____

_____

_____

_____

2. Is America Democratic or Communist?

_____

_____

3. Have politics ever played a role in other wars? If so, name some current or past.

_____

_____

_____

4. What do you know about the Cold War? Did Cold War politics play a role in American policies in Indochina?

Background and Causes

American involvement in Vietnam began after 1954. During World War II Vietnam was occupied by Japanese forces. In 1945 when the Second World War ended Vietnam was divided in two with Great Britain controlling the south and China controlling the north until Japanese troops could be rounded

up and returned to Japan. During this period Great Britain supported the return of the French to Vietnam. The French had controlled Vietnam (or Indochina) as a colonial possession before World War II. France fought a nine year war in Vietnam and was heavily supported by the United States government but in the end French forces were defeated at Dien Bien Phu in 1954, leaving the north in the control of the communist Viet Minh and their leader Ho Chi Minh.

After the French lost control of Indochina, the United States moved into the south of Vietnam hoping to help the South Vietnamese develop a democratic government based on American democracy. As time went

What year did American involvement start in Vietnam?

_____

_____

Background and Causes

on and the United States became more involved in Vietnam, American Cold War politics became more evident. They hoped to build a strong democratic government in South Vietnam that would keep the communist threat of North Vietnam from spreading through Southeast Asia. The Soviet Union, China, and their allies supported North Vietnam and their communist government.

In their efforts to establish a democratic government, the United States backed the leadership of Ngo Dinh Diem, a firm anti-communist. Diem led the country for nine years and it was during his presidency that the United States sent military and civilian advisors to work with and train the South Vietnamese Army and government officials. In the early 1960's the United States, under President Kennedy, continued to increase its' military support by sending more machinery, equipment and advisors. The Diem era ended in 1963 when he was assassinated by some of his military generals. Three weeks later, President Kennedy was assassinated in Dallas, Texas.

The new American president, Lyndon Johnson, felt that more aggressive action was needed in Vietnam. When two U.S. warships were attacked off the coast of Vietnam in August of 1964, the U.S. government passed the Gulf of Tonkin Resolution, granting the president broad powers of war. President Johnson ordered air strikes on North Vietnam, and in 1965 the first American combat troops arrived in Vietnam.

Background and Causes

1. Circle the word **TRUE** if the statement is TRUE or Circle the word **FALSE** if it is FALSE.

a) The French controlled Vietnam prior to World War II.

TRUE   **FALSE**

b) Vietnam was a democratic country.

TRUE   **FALSE**

c) The Soviet Union was an American ally.

TRUE   **FALSE**

d) The United States backed the leadership of Ngo Dinh Diem.

TRUE   **FALSE**

e) President Kennedy was assassinated in Texas during the Vietnam War.

TRUE   **FALSE**

f) Lyndon Johnson was less aggressive with the actions he took.

TRUE   **FALSE**

2. Complete each sentence with a word from the list.

leadership	democratic	Japanese	supported
South	defeated	nine	

During World War II Vietnam was occupied by _____ forces. During this
                                              a

period Great Britain _____ the return of the French to Vietnam. France
                          b

fought a _____ year war in Vietnam before being _____ in
              c   **d**

1954. The United States moved into _____ Vietnam hoping to help the
                                        e

South Vietnamese develop a _____ government. The United States
                                f

backed the _____ of Ngo Dinh Diem.
                g

Background and Causes

3. Unscramble the following words that all relate to the Background and Causes of the Vietnam War.

a. VEDDIDI _____

b. TRGEA IIATNRB _____

c. AICNH _____

d. ITICSOPL _____

e. CDEMOATIRC _____

f. UMCOMSNTI _____

4. What was the main idea behind the American Cold War policy involving North Vietnam and its allies, China and Russia?

_____

_____

_____

_____

5. Research the Gulf of Tonkin Resolution. What did it do for President Johnson? Was it an actual declaration of war? What powers did it give the President?

_____

_____

_____

_____

NAME: _____

Major Figures

1. Which president involved in the Vietnam War was assassinated on America soil?

_____

_____

2. Can you name the only U.S. president to resign?

_____

3. A. List as many former U.S. presidents as you can.

_____

_____

_____

_____

_____

_____

B. Now go to the classroom computer and see how many presidents you missed.

_____

_____

4. How many U.S. presidents were involved in the Vietnam War? Can you name them?

_____

_____

Major Figures

John F. Kennedy was born on May 29, 1917. He was the 35th president of the United States from 1961 until November 22, 1963 when he was assassinated in Dallas, Texas. Kennedy married Jacqueline Bouvier and had two children, Caroline and John Jr. He was a member of Congress from 1947 to 1953 and a senator from 1953 to 1960. Kennedy believed in fighting against communism and its spread. In order to accomplish this Kennedy and the United States provided political, economic, and military support for the government of South Vietnam. Under Kennedy 16,000 military advisors and Special Forces personnel were sent to Vietnam to help train and equip the Army of the Republic of Vietnam (ARVN).

Lyndon B. Johnson was born August 27, 1908. He was the 36th president of the United States. As the Vice-President he was sworn in as the President after Kennedy was assassinated. He remained in office until 1968. He was a member of Congress from 1937 to 1949 and was a senator from 1949 to 1961. Johnson also believed in the containment of communism but unlike Kennedy he felt that more

Who was the U.S. President in October of 1963?

STOP

_____

_____

_____

Major Figures

decisive action was needed in Vietnam. Under Johnson the United States sent the first American combat troops to Vietnam. He steadily escalated the ground war in Vietnam from 1965 to 1968 and by the end of 1968 there were around 550,000 American troops in Vietnam.

Richard M. Nixon was born January 9th, 1913. He was the 37th president of the United States. Nixon served as President from 1969 until he resigned in 1974, the only U.S. President to do so. Nixon also served as a member of Congress and as a senator. He served as the Vice- President to Dwight Eisenhower. As President, Nixon decided to pursue what was called "Vietnamization", where American troops would be gradually replaced by Vietnamese troops. Under Nixon American soldiers were steadily withdrawn until the last U.S. troops left in 1973. Congress also started cutting back funds and support for the war in Vietnam. Nixon was also remembered for ordering secret bombings in Laos and Cambodia to try and disrupt the supply routes of enemy troops on the Ho Chi Minh Trail, as well as sending U.S. troops into Cambodia.

General William Westmoreland was born on March 26th, 1914 and died July 18th, 2005. He graduated from West Point Military Academy and served in World War II and the Korean War. After becoming a General, he commanded American military operations in Vietnam from 1964 to 1968. He was the U.S. Army Chief of Staff from 1968 until 1972. Westmoreland believed that North Vietnam could be defeated by fighting a war of attrition, which meant wearing down your enemy by superior numbers. He had a great reputation as really caring for his troops.

Ho Chi Minh was the Prime Minister of the communist Democratic Republic of Vietnam from 1945 until 1954, and was the President of the Democratic Republic of Vietnam from 1946 until his death in 1969. Little is known about his early life however he did travel in Europe, the United States, and Asia while he developed his views on communism and Vietnamese independence. He led the Viet Minh against the French and defeated them at Dien Bien Phu, and led North Vietnam in the Vietnam War until his death in 1969. Ho's vision of a united Vietnam was realized in 1975 when North Vietnam defeated the South after the American withdrawal in 1973.

Major Figures

1. The following are multiple choice questions. Circle the answer that is correct.

a) Name the 35th president of the United States of America.
- **A** John F. Kennedy
- **B** Dwight Eisenhower
- **C** Lyndon B. Johnson
- **D** George W. Bush

b) He was both Vice-president and President of the United States of America.
- **A** John F. Kennedy.
- **B** Dwight Eisenhower.
- **C** Lyndon B. Johnson.
- **D** George W. Bush.

c) When did the war in Vietnam escalate and combat troops were sent to fight?
- **A** 1968
- **B** 1965
- **C** 1973
- **D** 1944

d) General William Westmoreland fought in these wars:
- **A** World War I and II
- **B** World War II and Vietnam
- **C** World War II, Vietnam and Korean War
- **D** None of the above

e) Ho Chi Minh's vision was to:
- **A** unite North and South and have it become a communist country.
- **B** split up the North and South so he could rule one.
- **C** travel to the United States and fight for American soil.
- **D** None of the above.

f) When did America withdraw from Vietnam?
- **A** 1998
- **B** 1965
- **C** 1973
- **D** 1975

g) What year was Ho Chi Minh's vision of a united Vietnam realized?
- **A** 1998
- **B** 1965
- **C** 1973
- **D** 1975

Major Figures

2. Circle the major figures below that had some involvement in the Vietnam War.

Admiral Yamamoto	Lyndon Johnson	George Bush
Bill Clinton	Ngo Dinh Diem	John F. Kennedy
Richard Nixon	Abraham Lincoln	Dwight Eisenhower
George Washington	William Westmoreland	Ho Chi Minh

3. What U.S. president was ultimately responsible for the American withdrawal from Vietnam?

_____

_____

_____

_____

_____

4. Give some reasons why you think the United States eventually ended their involvement in Vietnam.

_____

_____

_____

_____

_____

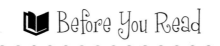

NAME: _____

Major Battles

1. Using a dictionary can you connect the word with the meaning?

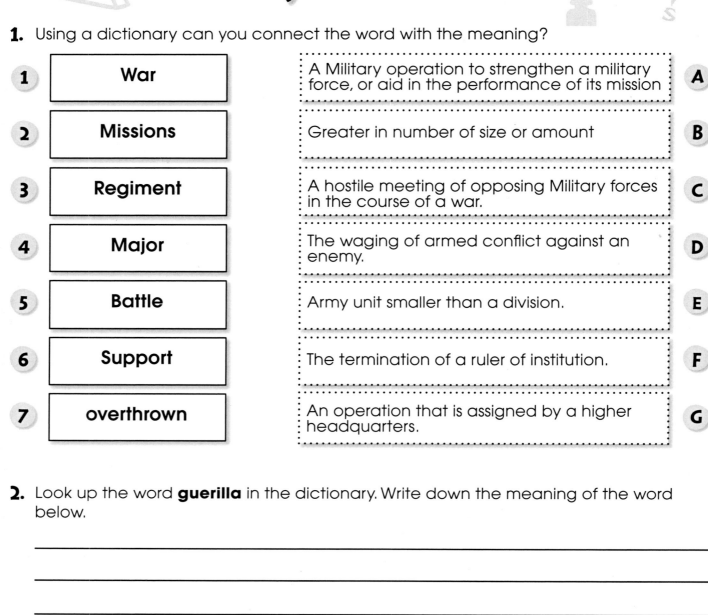

1	War
2	Missions
3	Regiment
4	Major
5	Battle
6	Support
7	overthrown

A Military operation to strengthen a military force, or aid in the performance of its mission	A
Greater in number of size or amount	B
A hostile meeting of opposing Military forces in the course of a war.	C
The waging of armed conflict against an enemy.	D
Army unit smaller than a division.	E
The termination of a ruler of institution.	F
An operation that is assigned by a higher headquarters.	G

2. Look up the word **guerilla** in the dictionary. Write down the meaning of the word below.

_____

_____

_____

3. Did the U.S. forces or the Viet Cong use guerilla tactics? Explain your answer.

_____

_____

_____

NAME: _____

Major Battles

There were many different battles and operations during the Vietnam War. Most involved large numbers of U.S. troops performing sweeps of certain areas searching for the enemy. These were called search and destroy missions. Three of the major battles are described below.

The battle of Ia Drang took place from November 14th – 17th 1965. The U.S. 1st Cavalry Division was specially trained in using helicopters as their main means of transportation. They were sent inland to Pleiku to help relieve Special Forces units under attack in that area. The battle began when two North Vietnamese Army (NVA) regiments attacked the Special Forces camp at Plei Me. The 7th Calvary landed troops on the battlefield using helicopters. American forces used heavy artillery and air support over two days and were able to defeat the NVA regiment. The NVA retreated losing more than 2000 men compared to U.S. losses of around 200 men. A day later when moving to a new location a couple miles away, U.S. troops were ambushed killing or wounding 280 Americans. In the battle of Ia Drang the U.S. was the clear winner in numbers killed, what they called the body count. The Americans learned that they had a clear advantage of mobility and superior firepower when used properly.

Khe Sanh was a remote base near the DMZ, or Demilitarized Zone, in the north part of South Vietnam. It was very strategically important. Khe Sanh was one of the highest points in the area and the American forces were able to watch the Ho Chi Minh Trail and roads in the area. U.S. Marines often occupied the base and then left it. In April and

When did the battle of Ia Drang take place?

_____

_____

Major Battles

May of 1967 a small force of Marines occupying the base encountered an NVA division and successfully defended the base from being overrun. On another occasion in 1968 the base at Khe Sanh was besieged by 40,000 NVA and Viet Cong (VC) troops. 6000 marines successfully defended the base over 3 months (January – March). American forces were able to relieve the defenders and the siege ended April 8, 1968. The U.S. lost 300 men and the NVA lost between 10,000 and 15,000 soldiers.

A whole series of major battles occurred during the Tet Offensive. During the Tet holiday and cease fire of January 1968 over 80,000 NVA and VC soldiers launched coordinated attacks in major cities and hamlets all over South Vietnam including Saigon and Hue. The government in North Vietnam expected the public to rise up and join in to overthrow the government in South Vietnam but this never did happen. After some initial victories, U.S. and ARVN troops were able to rally and push back NVA forces. Some of the most intense fighting was in the city of Hue. The NVA took over most of the city and U.S. troops had to retake it.

NVA/VC forces learned early in the war the results of fighting large pitched battles with American forces which had superior firepower, mobility and air support. The NVA and Viet Cong used guerilla tactics, using the jungle and terrain to their advantage. They tried to dictate where and when battles were fought. The NVA and VC developed massive tunnel and bunker systems to hide from U.S. forces. They used ambushes and struck at American forces and then would fade back into the jungle and into their hidden bunkers. These tactics were difficult for the American troops to handle. Their soldiers were for the most part very young- the average age of a combat soldier in Vietnam was 19. Vietnam was totally alien to them and there were no clear battle lines. The enemy was elusive and basically could be hiding anywhere and everywhere, ultimately causing low morale.

After You Read 📖

Major Battles

1. Circle the word **TRUE** if the statement is TRUE **or** Circle the word **FALSE** if it is FALSE.

   a) Khe Sanh was a major city in Vietnam.
   TRUE   **FALSE**

   b) During the 1968 Tet holiday cease fire, attacks happened in major cities.
   TRUE   **FALSE**

   c) Hue is a city in Vietnam.
   TRUE   **FALSE**

   d) The Ia Drang battle took place in November 1965.
   TRUE   **FALSE**

   e) Intense fighting happened in Hue.
   TRUE   **FALSE**

   f) American forces did not have superior firepower.
   TRUE   **FALSE**

   g) The average age of a Vietnam solider was 29.
   TRUE   **FALSE**

2. Number these events in the order in which they happened, from the earliest to the latest.

   ____ **a)** The American Government sends military advisors and equipment to South Vietnam.

   ____ **b)** The Siege of Khe Sanh.

   ____ **c)** The French army loses the Battle of Dien Bien Phu.

   ____ **d)** The Tet Offensive.

   ____ **e)** The Battle of Ia Drang takes place.

3. Imagine that you are a marine at the base of Khe Sanh while it is under attack. Write a letter home describing your experience.

   _____

   _____

Weapons of the War

1. Circle the word that does not belong?

A.	Helicopter	Tank	Soldier	Patrol Boat
B.	Bomber	Rice	Launcher	Weapon
C.	Agent Orange	Ground	Ocean	Air

2. Using your dictionary look up the word **weapon** and write its definition below.

_____

_____

_____

_____

3. a) In Vietnam the U.S. used a herbicide called Agent Orange to kill vegetation. Use a dictionary to define **herbicide**.

_____

    b) What kind of effects do you think this herbicide had on the environment and on people?

_____

_____

4. Make a list of the weapons you think may have been used in Vietnam. (Remember that more than guns were used).

_____

_____

Weapons of the War

When American involvement in Vietnam began in 1954 it was in a fairly limited role. The U.S. sent equipment and military advisors to Vietnam to help train the South Vietnamese Army (ARVN). While President Kennedy was in office there were around 16,000 military advisors and personnel sent to Vietnam.

One of the major contributions of the U.S. was the introduction of the helicopter in Vietnam. The UH-1 helicopter, known as the Huey by the troops, became the workhorse of the U.S. Army. Early in 1962, Operation Chopper involved American military pilots carrying over 1,000 South Vietnamese soldiers in helicopters to perform a sweep of a Viet Cong stronghold near Saigon. These were the first combat missions against the Viet Cong that American forces were involved in.

Weapons of the War

STOP

What was one of the major contributions the U.S. made in terms of Weapons of the War?

_____

_____

American forces in Vietnam were able to draw from a massive arsenal of weapons, from the mighty B-52 bomber right down to the bayonet. The primary weapon of the U.S. combat soldier on the ground was the M-16 rifle. The M-16 was lightweight and easy to care for. It could fire up to 700 rounds per minute on full automatic. U.S. troops also carried the M-79 grenade launcher and the M-60 machine gun- a larger light machine gun that could fire a continuous stream of rounds fed from a belt.

North Vietnamese Army (NVA) and Viet Cong (VC) soldiers used a version of the AK-47 assault rifle as their primary weapon. They were supplied by their communist allies, Russia and China. Both sides used mortars and artillery guns in combat. The U.S. forces also used a variety of vehicles on the ground including tanks.

Air support in Vietnam was crucial to the American forces. Along with the helicopters, the U.S. sent two aircraft carriers to the coast of Vietnam. The jet fighter/bombers aboard these carriers provided much of the air support for the ground troops as well as performing bombing operations all over Vietnam. U.S. aircraft were also used in Operation Ranchhand. Large areas of forest and jungle were sprayed from the air with Agent Orange, a herbicide, in order to clear away vegetation.

After You Read

Weapons of the War

1. Complete each sentence with a word from the list. The passage will reflect a true statement from this chapter.

NORTH	VEGETATION	RIFLE	1954
SOUTH	ORANGE	TANKS	HELICOPTER
PRIMARY	MILITARY	TRANSPORT	

The U.S. sent equipment and _____ advisors to Vietnam when

a
American involvement began in _____.

b
The _____ was a major contribution made by the U.S. The

c
helicopters helped _____ over 1000 _____

d   e
Vietnamese to attack the Viet Cong.

The U.S. soldiers had many weapons to choose from. The _____

f
weapon was the M-16 _____.

g
The _____ Vietnamese Army used a version of the AK-47 as

h
their primary weapon. U.S. soldiers also used _____. To clear

i
_____ the U.S. used Agent _____, an herbicide.

j   k

2. Circle the word **TRUE** if the statement is TRUE **or** Circle the word **FALSE** if it is FALSE.

a) American involvement in Vietnam began in 1945.

    TRUE   FALSE

b) Air support was not extremely important in Vietnam.

    TRUE   FALSE

c) While President Kennedy was in office there were around 16,000 military advisors and personnel in Vietnam.

    TRUE   FALSE

d) A major contribution made by the U.S. was the helicopter.

    TRUE   FALSE

e) The American soldier's primary weapon was the AK-47.

    TRUE   FALSE

f) The U.S. sent two aircraft carriers to patrol off the Vietnam coast.

    TRUE   FALSE

g) Agent Orange is a herbicide used to kill soldiers.

    TRUE   FALSE

Weapons of the War

3.   Explain why the helicopter was so important to the U.S. war effort.

_____

_____

_____

_____

_____

_____

4.   Finish the statement below by writing the letter that is missing from each set.

a) Early in 1962, ____ ____ ____ ____ ____ ____ ____ ____ ____ Chopper involved

          NPQ NOQ DFG PQS BCD RSU GHJ NPQ MOP

American military ____ ____ ____ ____ ____ ____ carrying over 1000

          OQR HJK JKM NPQ SUV QRT

South Vietnamese soldiers in helicopters to perform a sweep of a Viet Cong

stronghold near ____ ____ ____ ____ ____ ____.

          RTU BCD HJK FHI MNP LMO

b) The M-16 was light ____ ____ ____ ____ ____ ____ and easy to care for.

          VXY DFG HJK FHI FGI SUV

It could ____ ____ ____ ____ up to 700 rounds per minute on full automatic.

          EGH HJK QST DFG

The Role of the Navy

1. Have a look at a map of Vietnam. Where do you think the Navy would operate? Explain your answer.

_____

_____

_____

_____

_____

2. When you think of Vietnam you don't really think of the Navy. What kind of duties or missions do you think the Navy would have been involved in?

_____

_____

_____

_____

_____

3. Match each of the words below with its' meaning. You can use a dictionary to help.

a POW	_____ **A**	A nuclear powered aircraft carrier
b SEAL Teams	_____ **B**	a small fast boat used to patrol inland waterways
c blockade	_____ **C**	Special Forces branch of the Navy
d gunboat	_____ **D**	stopping the flow of supplies
e USS Enterprise	_____ **E**	Prisoner of War

NAME: _____

The Role of the Navy

The Navy also played a very important role in the U.S. war effort in Vietnam. The Navy had three major jobs. The first was to stop the flow of supplies by sea from North Vietnam from getting to communist troops in the South. The second was to provide artillery support from the big ships' guns. The artillery fire protected troops under attack as well as bombarded North Vietnamese and Viet Cong positions and bunkers. The third was to use smaller and faster boats to police and patrol the vast inland waterways and rivers. As well as patrolling the waterways, the Navy used the rivers to provide quick transport of troops and supplies into hard to reach areas. Naval forces in Vietnam were divided into two forces called the Blue Water Navy and the Brown Water Navy. The Blue Water Navy patrolled the deep waters off the coast of Vietnam and included battleships, cruisers, destroyers and the first nuclear-powered aircraft carrier, the U.S.S. Enterprise. The Brown Water Navy used patrol gunboats and other fast ships and boats to cruise the inland rivers and coastal seas. Brown water referred to the brown murky color of the waters that covered the country.

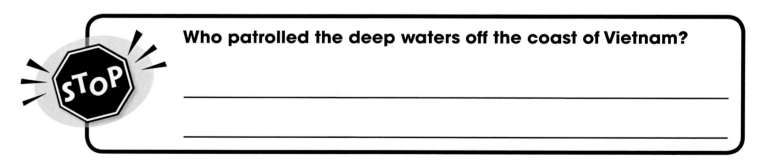

Who patrolled the deep waters off the coast of Vietnam?

_____

_____

The Special Forces branch of the Navy were called SEAL teams. (SEAL stood for Sea, Air and Land). SEAL teams were usually small units that went on covert or secret missions to gather information, conduct ambushes, capture Viet Cong agents or rescue POW's (Prisoner of War). They were highly trained and performed many dangerous missions in the Mekong Delta and elsewhere in Vietnam.

The Role of the Navy

1. The following are multiple choice questions. Circle the one that is correct.

A. The navy had three major jobs which were:
- a) patrol the coastal waterways to ensure ground soldiers safety and provide artillery support.
- b) stop flow of supplies, provide artillery support, use boats to police and patrol vast inland waterways.
- c) to transport the soldiers from south coastal water to the north coastal water bringing them supplies and artillery.
- d) None of the above.

B. The first nuclear-powered aircraft carrier was called:
- a) Deep Space Nine.
- b) The U.S.S. Enterprise.
- c) Voyager.
- d) The S.E.A.L.

C. SEAL stands for:
- a) secret air and land.
- b) south air and land.
- c) land, seal and ground.
- d) sea, air and land.

D. Brown Water refers to:
- a) the Brown River.
- b) the murky brown color of the inland waterways.
- c) the brown bombs found at the bottom of the water.
- d) Both a and b.

E. SEAL teams were usually:
- a) large groups.
- b) small groups.
- c) separate groups.
- d) single men.

F. POW stands for:
- a) Prisoner of War.
- b) Prison of the West.
- c) Prisoner in trouble.
- d) None of the above.

The Role of the Navy

2. Describe three major jobs of the Navy in Vietnam.

a) _____

b) _____

c) _____

3. (Circle) the word **TRUE** if the statement is TRUE **or** (Circle) the word **FALSE** if it is FALSE.

   a)   The Navy played a minor role in the Vietnam War.
       TRUE   **FALSE**

   b)   One of the major jobs of the Navy was to provide artillery support.
       TRUE   **FALSE**

   c)   The USS Enterprise was a diesel-powered submarine.
       TRUE   **FALSE**

   d)   The Special Forces branch of the Navy was called the Green Berets.
       TRUE   **FALSE**

   e)   The Brown Water Navy patrolled the deep ocean coasts off Vietnam.
       TRUE   **FALSE**

4. What is the difference between the Army and the Navy?

_____

_____

_____

_____

NAME: _____

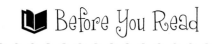

The War at Home

1. Can you think of some ways to communicate to your government that you agree or disagree with the war. Make a list of your ideas below.

_____

_____

_____

_____

2. Many of the protests that you read about were antiwar protests. Can you list some reasons why you think people did not support the war in Vietnam?

_____

_____

_____

_____

3. Using your computer or books, can you find any examples of rallies or marches in support of the war?

_____

_____

_____

_____

4. List some ideas as to how you would organize a protest.

_____

_____

_____

_____

NAME: _____

The War at Home

War is never a popular thing. The Vietnam War greatly divided the American people. As the United States became more involved in Vietnam, and more troops were being killed, anti war feelings began to grow. All across the country there were protests, marches and rallies. People started to question the government's motives and reasons for being in Vietnam. The majority of American people supported the president, but they also needed a reason for why so many American lives were being sacrificed in Vietnam.

There were famous marches and protests during the war. One protest in October of 1967 brought more than 100,000 people to Washington, D.C. The protestors marched on the Pentagon and were stopped by armed U.S. soldiers. Protestors put flowers in soldiers' gun barrels. Another infamous protest occurred in May 1970 at Kent State University. After demonstrations turned violent, the National Guard was called in. During the protest the National Guard fired into the crowd of over 2000 people, and four people were killed.

What did protesters put in soldiers' gun barrels?

_____

_____

The Vietnam War was the longest military conflict in U.S. history. By the end of the war more than 58,000 Americans had been killed and another 304,000 had been wounded. It is estimated that 3 to 4 million Vietnamese people on both sides were killed. It is believed that the financial cost of the war for the U.S. was close to $150 billion dollars.

NAME: _____

The War at Home

1. Unscramble the words below to find true statements reflected in this reading passage.

A. _____, _____ and
    esstorpt   ileslra

_____ broke out across the county.
hcesamr

B. _____ needed a _____ why so many
  anscimaer   aeonsr

lives were being _____.
                    slto

C. 100,000 were _____ to _____
            oughbrt   shongwtain

for a _____.
     testrop

D. Protestors put _____ in _____
          eolfwrs   rsslodie

gun _____.
    rrlseab

E. _____ turned _____ so
  strdemnooinsta   ntelvio

the National _____ was called.
        raudg

F. _____ people were _____ at a Kent State
  rouf   lldeik

_____ protest.
styireuvin

G. The Vietnam war was the _____ military _____
                    steongl   citflnoc

in U.S. history.

H. _____ 150 billion _____ was spent on the
  ylrouhg   drsallo

_____ War.
manietv

NAME: _____

The War at Home

2. Imagine that you are a protestor in the large march that took place in Washington D.C. In groups of three or four make up a large protest sign that you would carry during your march. Explain your sign to the rest of the class.

_____

_____

_____

_____

_____

_____

3. Do you think that the antiwar movement had a large or small impact on the United States government's policies on Vietnam? Explain your answer.

_____

_____

_____

_____

_____

_____

4. Which U.S. President was in office when the Kent State Tragedy occurred?

_____

_____

_____

_____

_____

NAME: _____

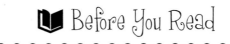

Remembering the War

1. Can you name any monuments that are in America today that commemorate a war? Name five monuments along with the war veterans that they honor.

_____

_____

_____

_____

_____

2. Using your classroom computer list at least five monuments that you did not name in the above question. Explain what war the monuments were built to remember and where you might find them.

_____

_____

_____

_____

_____

3. Why is it important to remember each war the United States has been involved in?

_____

_____

_____

_____

_____

Remembering the War

When the Vietnam War ended there were many issues facing the American people and veterans that returned home. The nation had been greatly divided over Vietnam and needed healing. Combat Veterans who came home felt unappreciated by the country and the ideal they had fought for. They were often treated poorly. Many veterans dealt with Post-Traumatic Stress Disorder (PTSD). It is a mental disorder caused when a person experiences something life-threatening or traumatic like combat. Many veterans couldn't deal with the drastic changes and life-altering events they witnessed in Vietnam and had a hard time returning to everyday life back in the United States. Many dealt with debilitating injuries and a changed society that scorned Vietnam veterans- soldiers who did nothing but long to return home after experiencing the horrors of war in a totally foreign and alien country. Even Hollywood, with films like Rambo, Platoon, Apocalypse Now and Full Metal Jacket have shown the more negative sides of the war. They portray American troops as lazy and uncaring, as well as focusing on other problems like a widespread lack of discipline, rampant drug use by troops, and atrocities that were committed against the enemy and Vietnamese civilians.

Another issue facing the United States after the war was the return of Prisoners of War (POW's) and soldiers listed as missing in action (MIA's). American troops and servicemen that were captured

Remembering the War

between 1964 and 1973 were sent to prisons or jungle camps all over North Vietnam, among which was Hoa Lo, called the "Hanoi Hilton" by the Americans. Conditions at these camps were horrifying and the Geneva Conventions of War, which called for the humane treatment of prisoners of war, didn't apply in Vietnam. Prisoners were often beaten and tortured to get information or false confessions of war crimes. Prisoners were often isolated and poor food and lack of medical care was standard. When the war ended in the spring of 1973, North Vietnam released all its POW's in what was called Operation Homecoming. Approximately 600 POW's were returned. However, many people believed that the Vietnamese still held American prisoners and that the U.S. government had abandoned them. There were more than 2500 people considered MIA at the end of the war.

 **In what year did the war end?**

_____

_____

As time went on Vietnam veterans began to be seen in a more positive way. One of the greatest memorials of the Vietnam War was unveiled in Washington D.C. in 1982. The Vietnam Memorial Wall, often just called "The Wall", is made up of 140 black marble panels that stretch almost 500 feet from one end to the other. The names of every American killed in the Vietnam War are engraved on the wall. It is a place meant for people to gather and share stories, grieve, and remember those who served and sacrificed their lives for their country.

NAME: _____

Remembering the War

1. Here are 7 words or phases that describe the "The Wall" in Washington D.C. Unscramble them.

oirlamem _____

melarb _____

senma _____

eirgf _____

raedvgne _____

iidecfcasr _____

lspnae _____

2. Circle the word that does not belong in the sections below.

a) Monument, The Wall, Statue, House

b) Platoon, Apocalypse Now, Star Wars, Full Metal Jacket

c) Face, Cry, Smile, Laugh

3. What does MIA stand for?

a) Men in Army

b) Missed in Army

c) Missing in Action

d) Murdered in Action

Remembering the War

4. Circle the word **TRUE** if the statement is TRUE **or** Circle the word **FALSE** if it is FALSE.

   a)   Combat Veterans returned to America and felt unappreciated.

   TRUE   FALSE

   b)   Once the POW's were returned there were no more soldiers missing in action.

   TRUE   FALSE

   c)   Currently there are no memorials for the Vietnam veterans.

   TRUE   FALSE

   d)   PTSD is a mental disorder.

   TRUE   FALSE

   e)   As time passed veterans were even less appreciated.

   TRUE   FALSE

   f)   Even Hollywood movies showed the more negative side of the Vietnam War.

   TRUE   FALSE

   g)   The Geneva Conventions of war allowed for the torture of prisoners.

   TRUE   FALSE

   h)   American troops called Hoa Lo prison camp the "Hanoi Hilton".

   TRUE   FALSE

5. The Vietnam Memoral in Washington D.C. has engraved:

   a)   the names of every American killed in the Vietnam War.

   b)   the names of every American who helped in the Vietnam War.

   c)   the names of every one killed in the Vietnam War.

   d)   None of the above.

Organize a Protest

Americans were greatly divided over their country's involvement in Vietnam. Many voiced their views through marches, rallies and protests.

As a class, or in small groups, organize a protest to the war in Vietnam.

Research the reasons WHY people were unhappy about the war.

HOW did the United States get involved?

WHAT was the turning point in the war? (Did the people support the war and later decide to protest against it or did they protest the war right from the start.)

WHO was to blame? If you are protesting the war there is usually someone or a group that you can blame. (often the government)

WHEN did the protest happen?

WHERE is the best place to hold your protest?

Also Remember to:

Write a speech about your reasons that you would give at the rally.

Make Protest signs and banners for your rally.

Think of some chants that you would use with the crowd.

These items would also require that you answer the questions listed above.

REMEMBER:

There were also rallies, and marches in support of the war, though they aren't as well known. Some groups could also do the same project but organize their rally in support of the war and troops.

At the end of the exercise you could hold a debate. Have one group debate the reasons why they are against the war and the other group can explain why it is important to support the war. Make sure you are prepared for any questions.

Diary of a Soldier

A great variety of American Forces personnel served in Vietnam. Each had their own unique experiences and daily routines. Imagine what their lives may have been like. Pick a person from the list below and research what their daily routine may have been.

Helicopter pilot

Soldier at Khe Sanh

Jet fighter pilot

SEAL team member

Prisoner of War

Navy Officer

Navy man on a patrol boat

Or a person of your own choosing

When you have picked a person and researched them write a three day diary of that person's experiences. You could talk about things like location, the terrain, what the weather was like, how they felt ... etc

Vietnam Collage

Let's have some fun!

A collage is a work of art created by placing various articles not usually associated with one another on a piece of paper.

Think about everything that you have learned about Vietnam and the War. Create a media based collage about the Vietnam War and the feelings that you have about it. You can use newspapers, magazines, pictures, words, pencil, pastels, colored pencils and crayons.

Remember! This is intended to be a fun exercise- show your creativity and express yourself! Think about your theme having to do with Vietnam and go with it. Take your time and really think about what statement you want the collage to make.

Web Navigation

Today you will be looking at a website that has to do with the Vietnam War. You are to navigate the website and answer the questions.

1. Log onto the computer, open a word document to record your answers.

2. Get on to the internet.

3. Go to the following website. www.pbs.org/battlefieldvietnam/. This is an excellent website about the Vietnam War.

4. Answer the following questions.

A. Go to "A Brief History". Find the section about the Gulf of Tonkin Resolution. What were the names of the two American warships that were attacked that resulted in Congress passing the Gulf of Tonkin Resolution?

B. Go to "Battlefield: Timeline". On what date did American helicopters arrive at docks in South Vietnam, along with 400 U.S. personnel to fly and maintain them?

   On what date in 1965 were the first bombing raids of Rolling Thunder flown?

C. Go to the "Guerilla" section. Find the section about the Viet Cong base at Cu Chi. How many miles of tunnels were found in the area and what kinds of things did they house?

D. Go to the "Air War" section. Find the information about the F-4 Fighter Jet. What is the maximum speed of the F-4? What is the weight of the aircraft?

E. Go to the "Khe Sanh" section. On what date did the NVA forces launch a massive attack, beginning the siege of Khe Sanh?

NAME: _____

Crossword Puzzle!

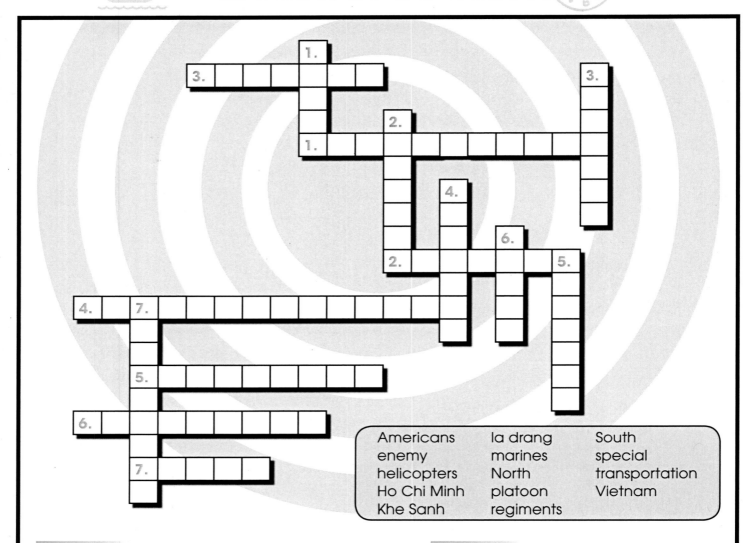

Americans	la drang	South
enemy	marines	special
helicopters	North	transportation
Ho Chi Minh	platoon	Vietnam
Khe Sanh	regiments	

Across

1. Air Transportation

2. These soldiers man the base at Khe Sanh

3. A movie about Vietnam

4. a tank or jeep

5. Army unit smaller than a division

6. Prime Minister of Communist party

7. _____ Pole

Down

1. Opposite of North

2. _____ War

3. Base near demilitarized zone

4. Large battle taking place in 1965

5. Forces with elite skills

6. Opposite of friend

7. People full of pride

Word Puzzle

K	H	L	M	O	M	R	D	E	V	A	R	G	N	E	R	D	N
M	I	P	R	S	N	E	A	S	T	O	R	I	E	S	T	Y	S
N	R	L	J	K	P	R	S	T	W	E	M	N	S	W	Q	S	H
P	S	T	L	A	S	V	E	T	E	R	A	N	S	C	D	Q	A
K	L	M	N	E	B	I	S	R	S	R	N	A	M	E	S	T	R
S	X	W	R	O	D	E	Q	Y	E	Y	T	S	T	I	A	P	E
O	D	Y	S	N	M	T	S	H	L	W	S	C	B	W	S	R	W
D	E	I	R	Z	Y	N	T	E	W	N	Q	E	L	R	T	W	V
I	T	D	O	A	C	A	M	D	Q	M	S	L	A	Y	R	X	A
S	A	C	B	B	G	M	N	C	Z	T	A	Y	C	Q	E	R	S
O	I	E	M	N	A	N	G	N	X	W	N	S	K	W	T	B	Q
R	C	N	A	T	I	O	N	A	W	T	N	U	S	N	C	N	D
D	E	S	R	Q	N	M	I	P	N	N	U	M	O	N	H	M	E
E	R	B	M	A	C	E	S	J	Y	L	R	O	O	P	X	D	N
R	P	T	A	C	D	A	S	M	M	I	T	N	Q	O	Y	E	O
M	P	Q	R	R	S	M	I	Q	N	A	C	P	C	S	U	L	D
N	A	N	B	A	W	S	M	P	L	I	O	S	D	I	Y	I	N
Q	N	W	L	T	S	R	Q	P	Y	O	M	U	A	T	X	E	A
V	U	T	E	V	E	I	R	G	E	U	B	I	W	I	Y	V	B
W	Q	P	D	S	A	B	N	M	Q	W	A	R	Y	V	E	N	A
M	E	M	O	R	I	A	L	S	X	R	T	O	R	E	R	U	S
S	A	C	Q	D	E	R	X	C	Z	K	R	R	P	O	N	Y	T
A	E	S	P	Y	L	A	C	O	P	A	W	A	C	T	I	O	N
T	O	R	P	E	O	P	L	E	A	T	Q	E	D	C	A	M	I

ABANDONED	GRIEVE	PLATOON	UNVEILED
ACTION	KILLED	POORLY	VETERANS
APOCALYPSE	MARBLE	POSITIVE	VIETNAM
BLACK	MEMORIALS	RAMBO	WALL
COMBAT	MISSING	SHARE	WAR
DISORDER	NAMES	STORIES	
ENGRAVED	NATION	STRETCH	
GATHER	PEOPLE	UNAPPRECIATED	

After You Read

Comprehension Quiz

NAME: _____

Part A

Circle the word **TRUE** if the statement is TRUE **or** Circle the word **FALSE** if it is FALSE.

1. The climate in Vietnam is hot all year round.
    TRUE   **FALSE**
2. The French were defeated in the Vietnam War.
    TRUE   **FALSE**
3. Ho Chi Minh was the Prime Minister of the democratic party.
    TRUE   **FALSE**
4. Guerilla tactics were never used in the Vietnam War.
    TRUE   **FALSE**
5. Orange Agent kills vegetation.
    TRUE   **FALSE**
6. The Navy had three major roles in Vietnam.
    TRUE   **FALSE**
7. The anti-war protests in the United States were always harmless with no violent rallies or marches.
    TRUE   **FALSE**
8. "The Wall" is a Vietnam memorial made of black marble panels.
    TRUE   **FALSE**

Part B

Circle the answer that is most correct.

1. Vietnam is found in:
    A.   Asia.   B.   Europe.
    C.   Africa.   D.   South America.

2. Democratic means:
    A.   the Government is appointed.
    B.   the Government stays in office until they decide to retire.
    C.   the people vote on their government.
    D.   the government is from the same family.

3. The 7th Cavalry troops arrived on the battlefield in Plei Me by:
    A.   jeeps.   B.   tanks.
    C.   U.S.S. Enterprise.   D.   helicopters.

4. 700 rounds per minute comes from a:
    A.   B-52.   B.   M-16.
    C.   M-79.   D.   M-60.

SUBTOTAL: /12

Comprehension Quiz

Part C

Answer the questions in complete sentences.

1. Can you name 4 topographical features found in Vietnam?   ②

_____

_____

2. How long was the U.S. involved in the Vietnam War?   ②

_____

_____

3. How did William Westmoreland believe the Vietnam War would be won?   ②

_____

_____

4. Name 3 types of antiwar movements that the American people used to help show the government how they felt.   ②

_____

_____

5. Name four types of water vessels the Blue Water Navy used.   ②

_____

_____

SUBTOTAL: /10

1. John F Kennedy

2. Richard Nixon

3. A. Any of the American Presidents

B. Computer assignments looking up all the presidents. They should be able to say that there were Presidents.

4. Three U.S Presidents – Kennedy/Johnson/ Nixon

(15)

John F Kennedy

(16)

3.
a. DIVIDED
b. GREAT BRITAIN
c. CHINA
d. POLITICS
e. DEMOCRATIC
f. COMMUNIST

4. They hoped to build a strong democratic government in South Vietnam that would keep the communist threat of North Vietnam from spreading through Southeast Asia.

5. It gave President Johnson authorization the use of military force in Southeast Asia. It wasn't an actual declaration of war. It gave him the power to take military action in Vietnam with approval from Congress

(14)

America's involvement started in 1954.

(11)

1.
a) TRUE
b) FALSE
c) FALSE
d) TRUE
e) TRUE
f) FALSE

2.
a) Japanese
b) supported
c) nine d) defeated
e) south
f) democratic
g) leadership

(13)

---

1. Answers will vary but one of the main differences is that a democratic Government is for the people. Democratic government's allow the people to choose their leader. A communist country does not. The leader is appointed and does not care what the people think.

2. Democratic

3. Yes. Almost all wars involved politics.

4. Accept any verifiable answer. Yes, Cold War Politics played a role.

(10)

Red River and the Mekong River

(8)

1.
a) FALSE
b) TRUE
c) TRUE
d) TRUE
e) FALSE

2.
a) CHINA
b) RED
c) VIETNAM
d) WESTERN
e) MONSOON
f) DRY

3.
a) Snow
b) hill
c) computer

(9)

1.
A.

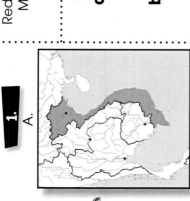

B. Answers will vary depending on where they choose

C. Answers will vary

2. Answers will vary

3. Answers will vary

(7)

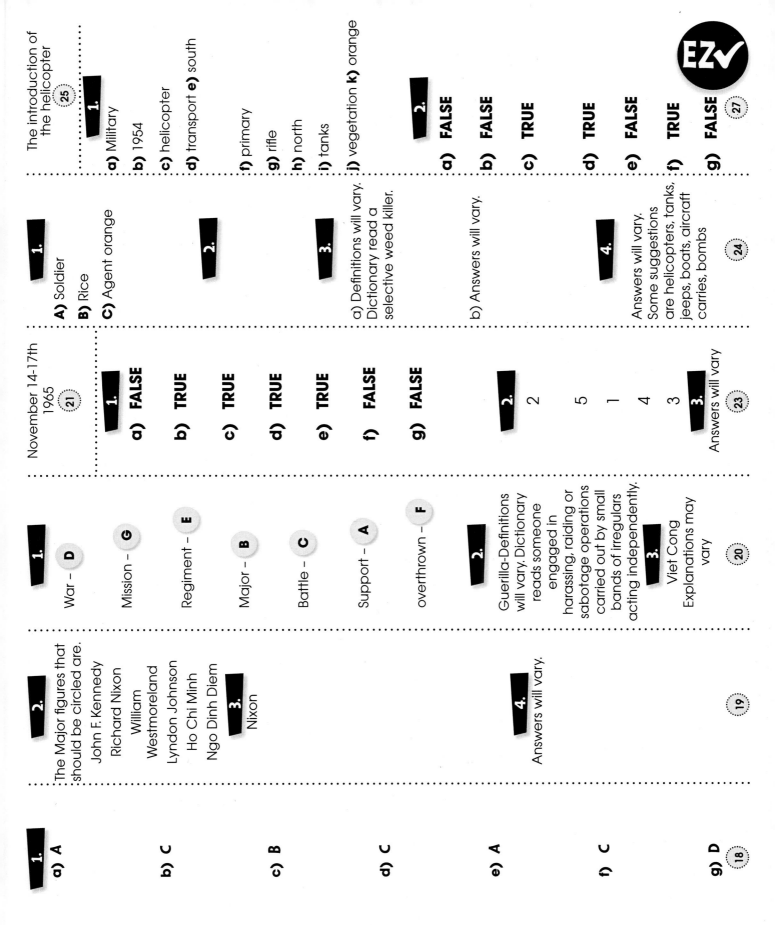

The introduction of the helicopter (25)

1.
a) Military
b) 1954
c) helicopter
d) transport e) south
f) primary
g) rifle
h) north
i) tanks
j) vegetation k) orange

2.
a) FALSE
b) FALSE
c) TRUE
d) TRUE
e) FALSE
f) TRUE
g) FALSE
(27)

1.
A) Soldier
B) Rice
C) Agent orange

2.

3.
a) Definitions will vary. Dictionary read a selective weed killer.

b) Answers will vary.

4.
Answers will vary. Some suggestions are helicopters, tanks, jeeps, boats, aircraft carries, bombs
(24)

November 14-17th 1965 (21)

1.
a) FALSE
b) TRUE
c) TRUE
d) TRUE
e) TRUE
f) FALSE
g) FALSE

2.
2
5
1
4
3

3. Answers will vary
(23)

1.
War – D
Mission – G
Regiment – E
Major – B
Battle – C
Support – A
overthrown – F

2.
Guerilla-Definitions will vary. Dictionary reads someone engaged in harassing, raiding or sabotage operations carried out by small bands of irregulars acting independently.

3.
Viet Cong
Explanations may vary
(20)

2.
The Major figures that should be circled are.
John F. Kennedy
Richard Nixon
William Westmoreland
Lyndon Johnson
Ho Chi Minh
Ngo Dinh Diem

3.
Nixon

4.
Answers will vary.
(19)

1.
a) A
b) C
c) B
d) C
e) A
f) C
g) D
(18)

1.
A) Protests allies
marches
B) Americans reason
lost
C) brought Washington
protest
D) flowers soldiers
barrels
E) demonstrations violent
guard
F) four killed
university
G) longest conflict
roughly Dollars
H) Vietnam
(35)

1. List will vary but some suggestions are:
Rallies
Parade
Posters
Marches
Letter

2. Answers will vary
Thought that they were losing lives for no good reason.
Lasted a long time

3. Accept any verifiable answers

4. Answers will vary
(33) Flowers
(34)

2.
a) Artillery support
b) stop flow of supplies
c) police inland waterways

3.
a) FALSE
b) TRUE
c) FALSE
d) FALSE
e) FALSE

4. Answers will vary
(32)

1.
A) b
B) b
C) d
D) b
E) b
F) a
(31)

1. Answers may vary interpretive

2. Answers will vary interpretive

3.
POW – E
SEAL teams – C
blockade – D
gunboat – B
USS Enterprise – A
(29)
The Blue Water Navy
(30)

3. Answers will vary

4.
a) operation
pilots
Saigon
b) weight
fire
(28)

Across:
1. helicopters
2. marines
3. platoon
4. transportation
5. regiments
6. Hochiminh
7. North

Down:
1. South
2. Vietnam
3. Khe Sanh
4. Ia Drang
5. special
6. enemy
7. Americans

46

4.
a) TRUE
b) FALSE
c) FALSE
d) TRUE
e) FALSE
f) TRUE
g) FALSE
h) TRUE

5.
a

41

1.
Memorial

Marble

Names

Grief

Engraved

Sacrificed

Panels

2.
a) house
b) Star Wars
c) face

3.
c

40

1.
Answers will vary

2.
Accept any verifiable answers.

3.
Answers will vary

37

1973

39

2.
Answers will vary

3.
Answers will vary

4.
Nixon

36

Word Puzzle Answers

Part A

1) TRUE
2) TRUE
3) FALSE
4) FALSE
5) TRUE
6) TRUE
7) FALSE
8) TRUE

Part B

1. A

2. C

3. D

4. B

Part C

1. Four Topographical features found in Vietnam are Mountains, Rivers, Forests and Jungles

2. United States was involved in the Vietnam War for 19 years

3. William Westmoreland felt the war could be won by wearing down the enemy by superior numbers

4. Three antiwar movements were rallies, marches and protests

5. The Blue Water Navy used battleships, cruisers, destroyers and the first nuclear powered aircraft carrier

(47)

(48)

(49)

The Vietnam War
Major Battles

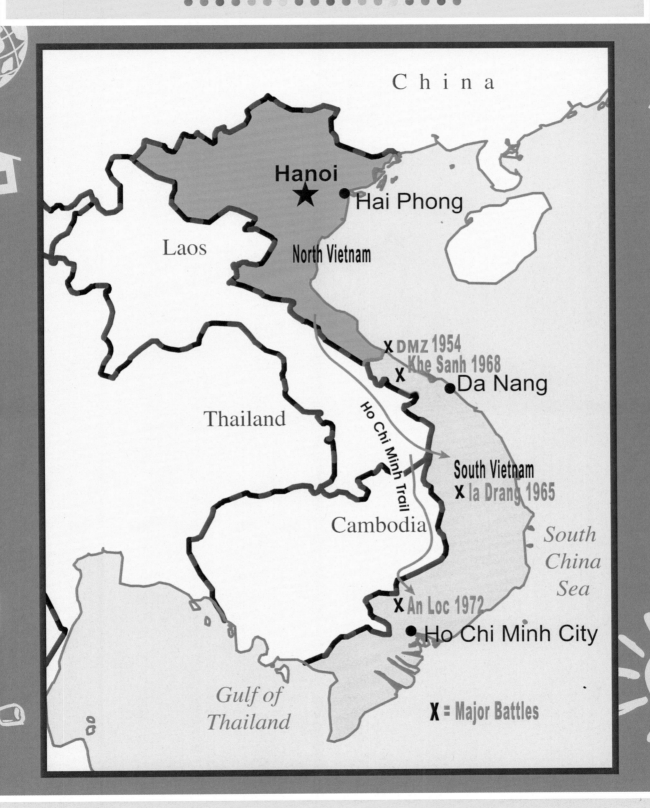

C h i n a

Hanoi ★ • Hai Phong

Laos

North Vietnam

X **DMZ 1954**
X **Khe Sanh 1968**
• Da Nang

Thailand

Ho Chi Minh Trail

South Vietnam
X **Ia Drang 1965**

Cambodia

South China Sea

X **An Loc 1972**
• Ho Chi Minh City

Gulf of Thailand

X = Major Battles

C-130 Airplanes lined up at Hue Phu Bai Battle of Hue-1968

The Vietnam War
Key Political Figures

J.F. KENNEDY
35th US President
1961-1963

L.B. JOHNSON
36th US President
1963-1969

R.M. NIXON
37th US President
1969-1974

HO CHI MINH
President of the Democratic
Republic of Vietnam
1963-1969

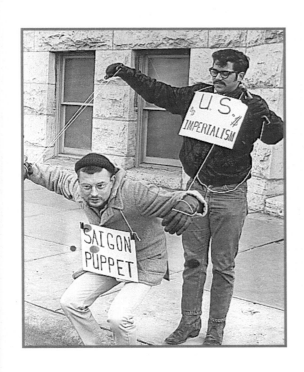

The Vietnam War
Memorial Washington DC